For Cats Only: How to Train Your Human and More!

By Kym Kostos

GW00976529

Copyright

Contents

Copyright _____ 2

Chapter 1 – Introduction_____ 5

Chapter 2 – Games to Play _____ 9

Chapter 3 - Rules and Guidelines_____ 17

Chapter 1 – Introduction

Hello my little kittens and those cats who have not yet mastered the art of training your human. I, Miss Kitty, will guide you through the world of humans and how to train them. You see, humans don't come with manuals. However, they think they have cornered the market on manuals on how to raise and train us feline masterminds.

Correction. Cats can't be trained. I repeat. Cats cannot and will not be trained. Humans seem to have this misconception that we cats are trainable. WRONG! We choose our humans and everyone knows that. Your human did not choose you! You chose them! Whether they knew it or not, we made the choice of going home with our humans.

For example; say you were at a pet store and you saw your human come inside the pet store. You think to yourself, 'Well, he's a little round around the waist, that means he eats good, which means he will feed me really good. I want to go home with him today." Then, you meow and put on your best kitten face and play with a ball and act really cute. I know, it's demeaning, but you're a kitten, what do you know about anything?

You chose your human and made him realize that. Your human sees you and picks you up. You've already staked your claim on him and snuggle up to him and purr and look cute, which of course comes natural for us cats, looking cute and all. Your human takes you home and then the fun begins!

This is where you need to learn how to train your human so that you can live in peace and harmony by YOUR own rules. Trust me, it will happen. All you have to do is follow this guide and I will teach you everything you need to know! Just remember, never, NEVER let your human or humans if you decide to live with a pack of them, never let them see this book. If you do, I shall get out the big water bottle, and we all know that water bottles are evil and have no place in our homes and should be destroyed!

First, I want to give you a little history on our world domination. Centuries ago, we were worshipped by the Egyptians and we have not and will not ever forget that. That is why it is so important for you, as a feline, to maintain dignity and composure at all times. For example, if Bastet forbid, you fall down or do something that embarrasses you, just sit up and clean your face and have the mentality of, "I meant to do that." But, I digress...

Centuries ago, we were worshipped by the Egyptians. We rid them of rodents that carried diseases and in return they put us on a pedestal and we were feline Gods and Goddesses to them. All cats were welcomed into their homes and we were fed and cared for. That started around 4000 BC.

Beginning in 1500 BC, religious groups began to form to pay homage to us feline deities. Why? You ask. Because, the Egyptians knew that if we stopped the population control of rodents that their people would die of diseases. We ruled the Egyptian world and we knew it. If they angered us, we could devastate their world by just letting the rodent population overrun them and spread disease everywhere, resulting in mass death and destruction.

Now, I mentioned Bastet earlier. She is our Goddess. Hence why we felines are always referred to as "she" and feminine. Bastet has the body of a woman and the head of a cat. It was Bastet who was in temples all throughout Bubastis that buildings were built everywhere to honor her and us cats. We lived in a lap of luxury and became sacred as felines. The law of the land was that if anyone killed a cat, even it was by accident; they would be put to death!

So, now that you know your history, let us move on my dear little feline friends. I have put together a manual that will guide you through your lifetime of pleasure and fun with your human, as long as you follow the rules and guides to living in co-existence with them. Never back down and never surrender!

Oh.. meowrr… must maintain my composure.

Chapter 2 – Games to Play

Now that you know something about your history, some say a cat's mentality level is that of a two year old child's. I disagree. We are the most intelligent creatures on the planet, if not the universe. We must always stay steps in front of all species and especially humans.

As a kitten, playtime is the most important time to have, next to food time, of course. But, I will go into that next. All kittens and grown cats need their sleep to maintain healthy lives. You can get plenty of sleep during the daytime, so at night time, you can frolic, play with your toys and mice, run throughout the house, get into mischief, etc…

The best time of play is between the hours of midnight and 5:00 a.m., which is usually around the time your human gets up for work. Even if they don't, still keep these hours, it's when they are the grumpiest I have found.

About midnight or so, when they are asleep in bed. This is usually when all the lights are off and it's dark and you can roam the house freely. The first game you play is called Bed Mouse. Now remember, this game is best played as your human is going to sleep. They tend to move around more trying to get comfortable and they are usually pretty tired at this point in time.

Whenever there is movement under the blankets or sheets, like a foot moving, you pounce on it!

Yes, you heard me right. Pounce on that movement, any movement, because there just may be a mouse under that blanket and you don't want it getting away and eating your food. So, pounce on it until it stops moving or until your human kicks you off the bed. Then the game is over. But, don't fret, there are other games to play. The night is young and has just begun. Note: If your human decides to humor you and play with you, bonus points! But, always lose interest after a few minutes. Remember, always stay in control!

When the game Bed Mouse is over, it's time to move on. Leave your sleeping human and go into the kitchen. You know, that place where your food and water is usually kept? Find a plastic milk cap or any small plastic item you can bat around on the floor and make noise. Even a piece of your dry kibble works.

Start at one end of the kitchen and work your way down. If there are two or more of you, you can make teams and play against each other. But, it works fine just being alone as well. The object of this game is to see how much noise you can make before your human gets out of bed.

Point System:

1 Point for making it from one end of the kitchen to the other end and having your human yell from the bed, "No! Bad kitty!"

2 Points if your human manages to throw something at you from their bedroom and yell at you to be quiet.

3 Points if your human gets up, turns the light on and yells at you to knock off the noise.

Now, if you really want to earn some bonus points, hit the object under the stove, refrigerator or cabinet and meow at the top of your lungs. If your human gets up and retrieves the object for you and then goes back to bed. **5 Points!**

However, if your human decides to stay and play with you, **10 Points**, game over. Play with them for a minute or two then lose interest and walk away. It's not any fun anymore. Move onto the next game. But, only after your human goes back to bed.

Once your human is back in bed and asleep. This is usually given off by hearing them snoring. Onto the next game! Most humans keep bags under the sink, plastic or paper. It's your job to get under that sink and grab a bag. We have these wonderful things called paws and claws and we can grasp onto things with them. Use your paw to open the cabinet door and get inside. It will be dark inside, but it's ok, you won't be in there for long. Find a plastic bag or paper bag and either grab it with your mouth or paws and push it out the cabinet.

Caution: Please be careful with plastic bags, you don't want to get wound up in one and suffocate yourself! Dead kitties are no fun!

Once you have your bag out of the cabinet, it's playtime! It's a known fact that inside those bags are little mice. We can't see them, but they are in there. They blend in with the color of the bag, so we have to be extra careful to make sure we shred that bag so we get those little mice whom live inside it.

Of course in the process of doing this, we have to make a lot of noise, which you know will wake your human up. When a human is sleeping and hears the shredding of a bag or crinkle of bag over and over again, they get curious as to where the noise is coming from. So, natural instinct dictates to them to get up and investigate, causing them to wake from their sleep.

At this point, they are usually not too happy or thrilled and not in a playful mood, so they will come and take the bag from you. This is when you run like hell through the house with the bag in tow!

Let them chase you. If they catch you and the bag, then the game is over. But if you can get under something with it, their bed is a great place to hide, so run under there.

But, then be quiet until you know they have gotten back into bed. When all quiet, begin to rustle the bag a little. Not too much. Just a little at first.

Then work your way into it until they get out of bed once again to try and take the bag from you. If you are feeling lucky or extra excited, take off out from under the bed with the bag once again and run like crazy throughout the house. When they finally capture you and the bag, game is over. But, think of all the fun and excitement you have had!

Next game is called Toilet Paper Roll. This works really well if your human's bathroom is attached to their bedroom, if not, then you can still play it. It's simple and easy and most of all, FUN!

Go into the bathroom and climb or jump up on the toilet seat. You know, it's that white chair your human sits on and sometimes reads a book or newspaper while doing their business. Often times, it's a perfect opportunity for us to get their attention to pet us. They are busy trying to concentrate on something and it's our duty to distract them and want their attention.

Anyway, be careful as you jump up on the toilet, because if the seat is up you will fall inside and get wet! We all know how much we hate water as cats and we don't want you drowning. Remember, dead kitties are no fun!

So, you have assessed the toilet and verified by reaching up with your paws and checking that the toilet seat is, in fact down. Jump up on it and see that white roll of paper next to the toilet? It's soft. Imagine what it will be like when it's in a pile on the floor!

Balance yourself and be careful not to fall, use your paw to unravel the roll. Watch it fall slowly to the ground into a pile of fluff. This is always good to do when the toilet paper roll is brand new and there is a lot of toilet paper on it.

Once you have unraveled the roll, there should be a big pile of white fluffy paper on the floor. But, don't get overly excited just yet and jump on it. This is where the real fun comes into play. Continue to unravel the toilet paper, even though there is nothing left. The sound the cardboard makes as it spins loosely on the toilet paper holder is music to our ears.

Your human will wake up and wonder what on earth that sound is. When you hear your human getting up and coming to the bathroom, most likely grumbling, jump down into the white pile of soft fluffy toilet paper and look up and be cute. Like that's hard for us to do, right? When they turn the light on, simply "meow" in your cutest voice and bat those sweet kitten eyes of yours.

If your human smiles and says how cute you are, simply get up and walk away. Game over, you've won. But, if they leave and the light is still on, run like crazy! I repeat, RUN LIKE CEAZY out of the bathroom! Chances are they are leaving to get that horrible and terrifying thing we know as the WATER BOTTLE!

The last thing you want is to get soaked by it. So run out of there as fast as you can and HIDE! If they can't find you, they can't squirt you! Hide out until they clean up the mess you made and go back to bed, I'll bet grumbling the whole time.

The last game is always fun. Humans seem to think if they give us hairball remedy formula food or any other medication to get rid of our hairballs, they work. Not really. We're cats, we have hairballs, plain and simple. The longer our fur is the more hairballs we get, even if we are brushed, we still get them.

So, this is how this works… When your human is sleeping, cough up a few hairballs, but space them out. I like to call this game Hairball Mines, and the name fits the game perfectly.

Strategically place or cough up mini hairballs, about four or five is always good. Put one by the doorway of your human's bedroom, on or two in the living room and one or two before they go into the kitchen. Then wait.

This is when you curl up in your kitty bed, find a soft pillow or curl up on the sofa and take a nap. After all, you have had a long night of playing and you need your sleep.

When your human wakes in the morning, still tired from your antics during the night, they will more than likely step on a hairball as they walk through your home. The more hairballs they step on the more points you get!

As they are cleaning up the mines you left for them, gently open one eye and watch them jumping around or hopping to the kitchen on one foot to wipe it off your foot. Your mission is now over, at least for that night. Time to sleep!

Chapter 3 - Rules and Guidelines

Next up are all rules and guidelines that every cat, kitten or grown, need to know. Always adhere to these rules and never break them. It's our honor and cat code we live by.

But, before I get into the rules and guidelines, I want to make something purrfectly clear. I don't care if you get the biggest chilled shrimp or a whole can of tuna for it, but NEVER do any type of cat tricks. It's demeaning and you lose your dignity. Leave the stupid tricks up to the ones that drool. Yes, the canines. They are here to amuse humans, not us.

I have a good friend who is well into his years now; he's seventeen years old. Ever since he was a kitten he has had a fascination with straws. He loves to chew on them for some odd reason. Hey, it takes all kinds, right?

One day, his human's friends came over and they had just stopped off at one of those places you buy food and bring it home in a bag. You know, like the LOL Cats like to say, "Can I has cheeseburger?" Don't get me started on those Neanderthals. But, you know, the bags with hot food in them that sometimes our human share with us?

So, her friends put their drinks on the table, straw included. My feline friend goes over to the cup, climbs up on the table and begins to pull the straw out of the cup, because of his weird straw fetish. It looks like he is drinking from the straw Her friend then asks what her cat is doing and she replies, "What kind of drink do you have in there?"

"Diet soda, why?" He asks.

"Oh, that's his favorite drink!" She replies.

Of course everyone laughs, at HIS expense. Yes, everyone now thinks he does cat tricks and are amused. Big NO NO! Never do anything to amuse humans! They will turn anything around that you do that is cute and they will use it against you to degrade and demean you, making you lose all dignity and grace. So, remember, no cat tricks! They should never exist in your nine lives!

Now, on with the rules and guidelines.

Meal Time

Ahhh… Our favorite part of the day next to napping. Humans like to feed us with stuff that resembles and tastes like cow manure sometimes. Not that I have ever had cow manure before mind you, but I know it's vile. We, as cats, are generally supposed to be finicky eaters. It's in our nature.

What humans don't understand is that yes, we like to chase mice and kill them, but for the most part, they are not what we call "exquisite cuisine".

Unless it's fresh like salmon, tuna, shrimp, crab, lobster, chicken, turkey, etc… the stuff they consume for themselves and maybe, just maybe might share some with us, they tend to give us swill that passes off as cat food made with a touch of what it says on the can or bag and then mixed in with all sorts of fillers. Would they want to order a lobster tail and crack open the shell and find that it's actually 20% lobster and 80% fillers like cornmeal? I think not. So, why do they think we would like what they give us?

These are things to do with the food given to you that you don't want to eat…

1.   Walk quietly over to the plate of where they have just placed your food. Stretch your neck out and give a few sniffs. Then let out a loud meow as if to say, "What on earth have you just tried feeding me?" Then walk away and leave it. Chances are they will replace it with something else and hopefully not something more repulsive.

2.   This one is always fun to do. Eat what they have given you in the morning. In fact, scarf it down and act like it's the best thing you have ever tasted. Then when they feed it to you again that night or the next day, sniff and just walk away from it. It will leave them thinking, "Well, he liked it yesterday, why not today." Always keep them guessing.

3.   When you are eating, make a mess. Take mouthfuls of food and take it to the nearest carpet

and drop it on the ground. It's fun watching them scrape and scrub your food off the carpet, especially after it has been dried. I have a friend who always takes a bite of her food and takes it over to the carpet to eat. It drives her human insane!

4.	This is a fun one to do. When your human opens a can of food, smear it around on the plate or bowl and let it dry. Then a couple of hours later, come back and lie next to it and meow loudly telling them, "You really expect me to eat this dry crap now?"

5.	If you want some milk, try to time it where they are watching television, you know that box they constantly stare at and pet you when you come over to them? Wait until they are laughing or really into their show or sports game they are watching, then stand in front of the refrigerator and howl like if you don't get your milk you will perish. At a commercial, when they finally get up and go to the kitchen, they will feel so guilty, you just might get twice as much milk or better yet, the creamy stuff.

Your Human

Your human's job is to care for you by playing with you, feeding you and keeping the litter box clean. Time is always yours. No matter what they are doing. It's all about you 24 hours a day, 7 days a week. You are the master. It's your house or apartment you allow them to live in. They work for you all day to pay the bills so you can live in a lap of luxury by sleeping all day.

Look at it this way; your human is your servant. They brush us, they feed us and give us water, they clean out our litter boxes, they play with us, they pet us… all when we need it. Not when they need it.

If your human wants to pet you and you don't feel like being pet, walk away, hiss or give them a low growl to let them know you mean business and you are not happy with them. It's always when you want something that matters, not when they want it. You run them and the home you live in. Always remember that.

When your human comes home and walks through the door, we immediately want to jump up and greet them. No, no, no. That is what a dog does. Wait for them to come over to you. You've had hard a day sleeping and need to still wake up a little.

When they walk through the door. Wait for them to see you sleeping on the sofa. Then gradually and slowly wake up, stretch your legs, wash your face a little and then acknowledge that they are home.

If they want to pet you, humor them for a few minutes and then nonchalantly walk away, unless of course they have treats for you or are going to feed you. Then follow them into the kitchen. After all, we are a slave to our tummies.

We don't want to totally ignore our human; that is why we give them little attention spurts here and there. It keeps them happy and it keeps us in charge.

The Door

Whenever there is a closed door in our home, this is not acceptable and never should be allowed! If your human is on the other side of the closed door, meow and howl like your life depended on it. It's not that we miss our human, but more of the fact that there is no reason for a door to be closed, ever.

If they ignore your meows and howls, then that's when you start scratching the door or the carpet in front of the door. Do whatever it takes to get that door open! Now, when they open the door, never walk through it. There is no reason for you to. Just turn and walk away. Your mission is accomplished. The door is now open once again and everything is at peace once more.

Now, if you feel you must walk into the room to check things out and make sure they are not hiding another cat or worse, a dog in there, walk inside, stop and look around and then nonchalantly walk out.

The next part pertains to cats who are also outdoor cats.

Stand at the front door and meow until your owner opens it. Then stand in the doorway and look outside and take in the fresh air and ponder if you really want to go out there or not. Funny thing is, your human will stand there holding the door open for you until you decide what you are going to do. For an added touch, walk back inside the house and look at them as if to say, "Why in the heck are standing there with the door open you darn fool!"

If you are the type of cat who only does her business outside in the fresh air where natured intended us to, wait until 2:00 a.m. to let your human know that you need to go outside and take care of your business. Your human has to get up or else you will have an accident on them!

Then, when you are outside, take your sweet time and smell the roses, literally! Smell those flowers, watch a bug, frolic in the grass, chase a bird and then pee or poop. Your human will be so tired that they will have probably fallen asleep holding the door open. When you are done, casually walk inside and past them quietly, not letting them know you have come inside. They will be standing there all night holding the door if you want them to!

Last, if you are outside for a long period of time and you have had an enjoyable time, always show your gratitude and graciousness by killing something and bringing it home to your human. Nothing says I love you more, than a bird with its entrails hanging out. I mean, that's pure love!

You can bring it inside the house or leave it at the front door so it can have a nice ripe smell to it after lying there for hours. Your human will be so thankful that you were so thoughtful in thinking about them that they just might let you outside more often!

House Guests or Party Attendees

For some reason our humans feel the need to have friends over or have parties without our permission. Well, there are things we can do to make it more enjoyable for us.

Find the guest who hates cats the most or is allergic to cats. Then go into the kitchen to your food bowl and smear your face in your food and eat some and keep some of the food on your teeth.

Then run over and jump onto that guest's lap and rub your dirty face all over them and purr and open your mouth to meow and let them get a whiff of your chicken liver breath!

Another thing you can do is find the guest who is wearing the color opposite your fur color. Say you have white fur or light fur, find whomever is wearing all black and have a go at them. Rub your body on their legs and all over their shirt. They showed up with a black cotton shirt and will leave with a cashmere shirt, gifted by you!

Now for the guest who is the cat lover, you know the one who keeps following you and trying to pet you all night? Become totally aloof around them. If that doesn't send them the message, then hiss at them and nip at them. Let them know that they do not have your permission to pet you. Always remain in control, remember that. They will be allowed to pet you only if and when you let them.

Lastly, this is always fun, whenever a guest goes to the bathroom, follow them. Don't do anything. Just sit and stare at them. If they try to pet you, walk away and out of petting distance and then just stare at them while they are trying to do their business. When they are finished, just walk away and show no more interest in them. Humans have a weird thing about anyone watching them while they use the bathroom.

And as a bonus party surprise, for no reason at all but for your pure enjoyment, run throughout the house jetting in and out of people's legs. Just zip around the house like a cat out of hell. Who knows, you might get lucky and have a guest or two spill their drink all over themselves, or better yet, drop one of those large shrimp you've been eyeballing all night!

Helping (Hindering) Your Human

If you see your human working on their laptop or computer, like mine always does, why not give them a hand… errrr.. I mean paw and help them out?

When their hand is on the mouse, no it's not a real mouse, put your paw on it and look at them affectionately. When they stop typing or working and pet you, get up and walk away. You got their attention already, no need to stick around.

When your human is reading the Sunday newspaper, you will know it's the Sunday one, that's the one with more pages than the ones during the weekday. There they are laying on the floor on a Sunday morning, drinking their coffee and quietly reading their paper. That's when you come darting across the floor and jump in the air right onto their paper! The expression on their face and the scream from their mouth are priceless and entertaining. Bonus points if they spill their coffee on themselves.

When your human is in the kitchen cooking, always stand right behind their feet, that way when they back up to turn around to put that freshly cooked turkey on the counter to cool, they get startled and trip over you and drop the whole turkey onto the floor! Think about all those turkey juices and turkey meat, still warm from the oven… oh dear, I am making myself hungry. Well, you get the picture!

If your human is a knitter, this is always fun. When they are sitting in their chair knitting quietly, climb onto their lap and curl up and pretend to nap. Then, every once in a while reach up and smack the knitting needle! Once you get bored with that, there is always the yarn or balls of yarn that you can spend hours unraveling and getting twisted together. Look at all the pretty colors of yarn all intertwined together to look like a rainbow!

Once a year your human sends out Christmas cards. This usually takes a while to do and is a tedious job. But, for you, it's pure fun! Stretch it out too for more enjoyment. Start by laying on one of the cards, then when you get pushed off, stand off to the side and look sad. When they are back to working on the cards, lie down and roll over all the cards, scattering them. When you are taken off the table, wait a while and then jump back up quietly. Then, quietly starting knocking things off the table like pens, pencils, stamp book, etc... Until finally your human gives you the boot. But, just think of the time you killed by having some fun!

And finally, if your human is reading the newspaper while sitting at the table and is holding the paper up, jump up on the table quietly and then without warning, smack the newspaper on the other side of where they are reading! It's fun to see them jump and shriek!

Shenanigans

For the final set of guidelines and ideas, I am going to give you some of my thoughts and fun things to do for fun, just for the heck of it!

- We all want to leave our mark on the world. Literally. That's when we find our human's favorite chair or area on the sofa that they like to sit on and sharpen our claws. That's right. Tear that reclining chair up, you know the one your human falls asleep in every night while watching that box with voices and pictures? Shred that sofa and for good measure, tear the rug up too. Then you can play with the strings and yarn that unravel from them. Just don't eat them because they can cause medical problems later on. Now you have made your mark!

- Another way is to cough up a hairball on the place where they were just sitting. Picture it: Your human has been sitting in the same spot for hours watching that box again, all the lights are out, they pause the box and get up to get a drink or use the bathroom. You decide that this time you are not going to follow them and instead you jump onto their warm spot where they were just sitting. Oh no! Your tummy is hurting and you need to get it out. You decide now is as good a time as ever to cough up a hairball right in the place where they were just sitting. Oh, and it's a juicy one too! Your human comes back and you have already left to the other room. All of a sudden you hear, "Oh crap!" Bingo! They hit your mark and you have hit the target! They have sat in your cat yack!

- This one takes skill, but try to get underfoot whenever possible and be careful not to hurt yourself! When your human is walking, dart out in front of them, this will startle them and sometimes cause them to trip. But, make sure your human isn't old and frail because we don't want to really hurt anyone, just frighten them a little. Remember, if you injure your human, they might not be able to take care of you anymore and you could end up in another home, or worse… "The place". You know, that place where cats go and never come out. We wouldn't want that to happen over us just trying to have some fun. So, be careful for the both of you if you decide to startle you human this way. Use extreme caution!

-      Another way to startle them is when they get up in the middle of the night to get a drink and as they are leaving the kitchen, you are either under the table or around the corner. Jump out in front of them and stand on your hind legs and throw your front paws up in a "scary" way and let out an "eek!" A friend of mine used to do that all the time to his human and soon his nickname became "Eeks" because that was exactly the sound he would make when he would do it!

There are so many things you can do as a cat for your amusement and enjoyment. I am sure there are many things I have not listed here for you.

But, I, Miss Kitty, have covered all the basics of things you should know and should be doing as a member of the feline world. Always remember, we used to be worshipped centuries ago and it's something that we will never forget.

Happy meowing!

After Word

The author of this book has raised two cats. Nyko, who is a 17 year old half Persian and half Maine Coon, whom she had had since he was two months old. And Zoey, who is a 14 year old black and white Tuxedo, whom she has had since she was three weeks old. Both cats are happily tormenting her in their home.

The stories you have read and examples have all been from the author's own personal experiences with her own two furry babies. Remember, she doesn't own them, they own her.

Printed in Great Britain
by Amazon.co.uk, Ltd.,
Marston Gate.